EPIC Leader II

Advanced Discipleship Training

Dave Park, D.D. & The Infusion Team

His Passion Publishing

Infusion Ministries

2021

We highly recommend you watch the free leadership videos which accompany this material. You can find a link at the bottom of the 'EPIC Videos' page on our website at infusionnow.org.

First Printing: 2016
Cover Design by Meghan Hamby
Current edition: 2021
Interior designed and edited by Kristie Kroschel and the Infusion staff.

Infusion Ministries is a national and international, interdenominational organization based in Knoxville, Tennessee. The purpose of Infusion Ministries is to awaken identity and establish freedom in the body of Christ. Our staff provides training and counseling through seminars, conferences, workshops, and resources with an emphasis on equipping pastors and small group leaders to do the same. We hope and pray that we will have the privilege to serve you and conduct one of our life-changing conferences or seminars for your group. Infusion Ministries is not a long-term counseling center. Through biblical truths and resources, we encourage and help believers in their walk with God.

Infusion Ministries
P.O.Box 22087
Knoxville, TN 37933
865-966-1153

infusionnow.org

CONTENTS

Forward

Welcome to this Infusion Ministries EPIC Leader II Training. This training is a continuation of the EPIC Leader I training and is for those who desire to help others claim their personal freedom in Christ. In the EPIC Leader II training, the focus will be on discipleship and how to disciple others in their walk with Christ. Paul said, "We proclaim him, admonishing and teaching everyone with all wisdom, so that we may present everyone perfect in Christ. To this end I labor, struggling with all his energy, which so powerfully works in me" (Colossians 1:28-29).

Within this training, you will learn the three levels of discipleship. We have provided a discipleship model to help you teach the identity and freedom materials in your area of ministry. Thank you for joining us. If we can serve you in any way, please let us know. Please visit us at infusionnow.org or call us at 865-966-1153.

Blessings,

Dr. Dave Park

Thanks for leading others to the truth that will set them free!

"If you abide in my word, you are truly my disciples,
and you will know the truth, and the truth will set you free."
John 8:31-32

Introduction

The apostle Paul revealed the <u>essence of his discipleship ministry</u> and <u>identity-based spiritual formation</u> in Colossians 1:28-29 when he wrote:

> *"We proclaim him, admonishing and teaching everyone with all wisdom, so that we may present everyone perfect in Christ. To this end I labor, struggling with all his energy, which so powerfully works in me."*

Our purposes in discipleship counseling and identity-based spiritual formation are the same—to present everyone complete in Christ. This is accomplished through preaching the gospel, warning about sin and its consequences, and teaching the truth. It is hard work, but we have the confidence that God's powerful energy is at work in and through us as we trust him.

Paul gives us further insights into the process of bringing men and women into spiritual maturity in Colossians 2:6-10.

Neil T. Anderson uses Colossians 2:6-10 to outline three key levels of spiritual formation in his book, *Discipleship Counseling.*

Level one - <u>being rooted</u> in Christ → *fullness*

Level two - <u>being built up</u> in Christ

Level three - <u>walking</u> in Christ

Understanding the conflicts to growth and maturity at these key levels is important in helping others grow spiritually.

Level One:

"...rooted and built up in him...and you have been filled in him,"
(Colossians 2:7,10)

A proper understanding of our identity in Christ is foundational to our spiritual growth. We are saved by faith in Jesus, and we are instructed to walk by faith in him. However, we cannot walk by faith if we do not have the right belief system. A distorted picture of who we are as Christians will result in a wrong belief system. A wrong belief system will result in wrong emotions and actions.

A person who does not have a clear understanding of who they are as a child of God will automatically seek to have their legitimate needs met through the world and the flesh. They will be easy prey for the temptations, accusations, and lying deceptions of the devil. It is impossible to live consistently in a way that is inconsistent with how you perceive yourself.

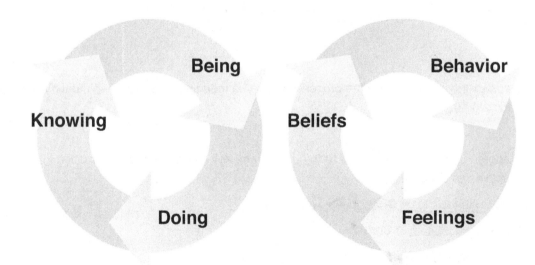

*In Romans 6, Paul outlines all three levels of spiritual formation: knowing, being, and doing. He gives us an outline for discipleship based on our identity in Christ. Paul's three-fold process takes us from the inner to the outer person, aligning the believer with spiritual truth and an abiding relationship with Christ. It begins with **knowing** one's identity in Christ (Romans 6:3-10), then believing it is true (Romans 6:11). Believing means that the truth has become a part of who we are: our very **being**. Finally, we yield or present ourselves to God, and our actions (**doing**) are conformed to Christ's desires (Romans 6:12-14).*

✱Born Again but, no knowledge

Identity Based Formation - Level 1 Conflict and Growth Chart *(Assurance of salvation)*

LEVEL 1 *Rooted in Christ*	Conflicts	Growth
Spirit *(soul level)*	**Lack of salvation or assurance** *Ephesians 2:1-3*	**Child of God** *1 John 3:1-3; 5:11-13* Lead them to Christ or give them assurance of salvation
Mind	**Darkened in their understanding** *Ephesians 4:18*	**Renewed mind** *Romans 12:2; Ephesians 4:23* Guide them to a true knowledge of who they are in Christ
Emotions	**Fear** *(1st neg emotion in the bible)* *Matthew 10:26-33* *When the lie is exposed it leaves... they can renounce & be free*	**Freedom** *Galatians 5:1; 1 John 4:18* Teach them the fear and love of God instead of the fear of man or Satan
Will	**Rebellion** *1 Timothy 1:9; Matthew 16:24* *Submit to authority &*	**Submission** *Romans 13:1-2* Expose the ways they have been "Playing God" or rebelling against his authority (including human authorities)
Relationships	**Rejection** *1 Peter 2:4; Ephesians 2:1-3* *Forgiving those who rejected but, also accepting the love of the father*	**Acceptance** *Romans 5:8; 15:7* Encourage them to receive and internalize God's love, acceptance, and affirmation, which is the foundation for free living in Christ

Adapted from *Discipleship Counseling*, by Anderson, N.T., 2003, p. 123, Ventura, CA: Regal Books.

Submit

Level Two:

"...and built up in him and established in the faith"
(Colossians 2:7)

The goal of Level Two counseling is to help people adopt God's purpose for their lives: sanctification (growing up into Christ-likeness).

Scripture teaches:

"For this is the will of God, your sanctification" (I Thessalonians 4:3).

"But like the Holy One who called you, be holy yourselves also in all your behavior: because it is written, 'You shall be holy, for I am holy'" (I Peter.1:15,16).

"For whom he foreknew, he also predestined to become conformed to the image of his Son" (Romans 8:29).

"But the goal of our instruction is love from a pure heart and a good conscience and a sincere faith" (I Timothy 1:5).

Our sense of self-worth as believers is found in our identity as children of God and is experienced as we grow in grace. Our sense of worth is not found in our appearance, performance, popularity, or possessions. Nor is our worth found in what talents, spiritual gifts, or fruitful ministries we might have. Those things are not equally distributed among Christians. Our worth is found in who we are (our identity) and who we are becoming (our character) in Christ. These two things are available to everyone!

IDENTITY INDICATORS

In Christ We Experience	Without Christ We Experience
Acceptance (Romans 5:1, 8,15,17)	Rejection (Ephesians 2:1-3)
Belonging (1 Corinthians 6:17)	Alienation (Ephesians 4:18 KJV)
Purpose (2 Corinthians 5:17-18, Colossians 3:4)	Meaninglessness (Ecclesiastes 1:2)
Power (Philippians 4:13)	Weakness (Psalm 27:1)
Authority (Acts 1:8)	Timidity (2 Timothy 1:7)
Submission (Romans 13:1-2)	Rebellion (1 Timothy 1:9)
Provision (Philippians 4:19)	Worry (1 Peter 5:7)
Guidance (Romans 8:14)	Being Lost (Hebrews 5:11-14)
Security (Romans 8:31)	Fear (2 Timothy 1:7; Matthew 10:26-33)
Significance (John 15:1,5)	Inferiority (Romans 8:37)
Peace (Galatians 5:22)	Confusion (1 Corinthians 14:33)
Freedom (Galatians 5:1)	Bondage (1 John 4:4)

Identity Based Formation - Level 2 Conflict and Growth Chart

LEVEL 2 Built up in Christ	Conflicts	Growth
Spirit	**Walking according to the flesh** *(out of harmony with God)* *Galatian 5:19-21*	**Walking according to the Spirit** *Galatians 5:22-23* Teach them how to walk in the Spirit
Mind	**Wrong beliefs or philosophy of life** *(resulting in ungodly goals)* *Colossians 2:8*	**Rightly handling the word of truth** *2 Timothy 2:15* Encourage a consistent habit of renewing their minds through biblical truth
Emotions	**Anger** *Ephesians 4:31* **Anxiety** *1 Peter 5:7* **Depression** *2 Corinthians 4:1-18*	**Joy, Peace, Patience** *Galatians 5:22* Unleash the fruit of the Spirit by renouncing fleshly goal setting that fuels anger, anxiety, and depression
Will	**Lack of self-control, compulsiveness** *(being compelled by forces other than the Holy Spirit)* *1 Corinthians 3:1-3*	**Self-control** *Galatians 5:23* Encourage habits of self-control
Relationships	**Unforgiveness** *(harboring bitterness)* *Hebrews 12:15*	**Forgiveness** *Ephesians 4:32, Colossians 3:13* Teach and help them to forgive others from the heart

Handwritten annotations:
- Show how to get out of walking in the flesh.
- Helps correct in PJ
- Must get in the word of God.
- Huge issue in culture today
- → Faith/Trust
- Spending / Boundaries / Relationships

Adapted from *Discipleship Counseling*, by Anderson, N., 2003, p. 123, Ventura, CA: Regal Books.

Level Three:

"...as you received Christ Jesus the Lord, so walk in him."
(Colossians 2:6)

The goal of level three counseling is to help people function as children of God at home, at church, and in their communities. The reason for this emphasis is that God's work in our lives takes place primarily in the context of committed relationships. We learn patience, kindness, honesty, forgiveness, faithfulness, etc. through interaction with other people. It is hard to be phony in a committed relationship because true character always reveals itself over time. Put another way, living maturely in the Lord is no easy task surrounded by the same imperfect people day after day.

Have to go through the process

In our zeal to correct people's behavior, it is easy to skip level one and two counseling and jump right into the practical "how-to's" of life. However, if we ignore the natural growth process, we can easily fall into legalism or some form of Christian behavior modification. We must help people establish the proper belief system first (based on God's character and their identity in Christ) before counseling them regarding their behavior.

• *People who find their identity in Christ & freedom heal from their wounds rather rapidly.*

The order of Scripture is first knowing (cognitive), then being (affective), and finally doing (volitional).

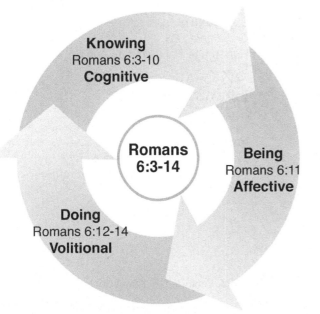

Knowing
Romans 6:3-10
Cognitive

Romans 6:3-14

Being
Romans 6:11
Affective

Doing
Romans 6:12-14
Volitional

The New Testament epistles have given us the model for instruction:

first, theology *to know* and *believe* (e.g., Ephesians 1-3, Colossians 1,2 and Romans 1-8)

then practical application *to do* (e.g., see Ephesians 4-6; Colossians 3-4 and Romans 12-16).

Encouraging people to walk in Christ involves teaching them to use their spiritual gifts and God-given talents and intellect to serve one another and be a positive witness in the world.

unstand the spiritual battles & know how to walk through valley

Identity Based Formation - Level 3 Conflict and Growth Chart

Level Three Walking in Christ	Levels of Conflict	Levels of Growth
Spirit	Insensitive to the Spirit's leading *Hebrews 5:11-15*	Led by the Spirit *Romans 8:14* Teach them to hear and obey the voice of God and not just live by feelings or rational processes
Mind	Pride → Check self *1 Corinthians 8:1* 2. Cor. 26 (king Uzziah)	Complete, equipped for every good work *2 Timothy 3:16-17* Help them forsake self-reliance and build confidence in God and his equipping work.
Emotions	Discouragement, sorrow, and boredom *Galatians 6:9*	Contentment *Philippians 4:11* Help them learn to be content joy and contentment in whatever circumstances they are facing
Will	Undisciplined lifestyle *2 Thessalonians 3:7,11*	Disciplined *1 Timothy 4:7-8* Guide them into godly discipline which is much more important than physical discipline
Relationships	Selfishness *Philippians 2:1-5;* *1 Corinthians 10:24*	Devoted to one another in brotherly love *Romans 12:10; Philippians 2:1-11* Point them to a Christ-centered lifestyle of generous, self-sacrificing love

Grounded

Adapted from *Discipleship Counseling*, by Anderson, N., 2003, p. 123, Ventura, CA: Regal Books.

Know king & priest → but always come hungry

Final Thoughts on the Process of Identity-Based Spiritual Formation

Many believers often suffer from spiritual ignorance, amnesia, or deception from the enemy when it comes to understanding their identity. They either do not know or have forgotten who they are in Christ. Also, the enemy wants desperately to keep them in the dark about their true identity in Christ. As a result, their self-image is derived from the wrong source. Using a variation of Luke 9:18-20, we can ask of ourselves three fundamental questions:

Who do you say that you are?

Who do people say that you are?

Who does God say that you are?

Too often, our sense of identity is based on our answers to the first two questions rather than the third. When we allow ourselves or those around us to determine who we are, we will unavoidably arrive at unbiblical conclusions and base our sense of personal worth on the wrong things. As believers in Christ, our identity must not be based on what people say but on what God says of us. God says that he unconditionally loves and accepts us regardless of how we feel or perform (Romans 5:8). He tells us that we have become "united with him [Christ] in the likeness of his death" and that we will also be united with him "in the likeness of his resurrection" (Romans 6:5).

Adapted Johari Window Graph

God sees the whole picture, and he will reveal the hidden things and disclose the motives of each heart when he is ready. Therefore, we must wait on the Lord for the timely revelation of what only he sees.

		COUNSELEE	
		You See	**You Don't See**
C O U N S E L O R	**I See**	Common Knowledge (You can see the problem and everyone else does as well)	Wisdom Counsel (You are open to hearing about your blind spots)
	I Don't See	Intimate Trust (You reveal yourself to a trusted friend who keeps a confidence)	God Alone Knows and must Reveal (Abiding in Christ and hearing from God's Word and Spirit)

Growth Possibilities

We encourage people to set aside pride and fear in order to honestly share the things they see in themselves that others don't see. This occurs best in the context of committed, accepting relationships.

"Dropouts" (see chart) tend to stay away from the people and places causing them to fall under conviction. One of the enemy's greatest ploys is to isolate believers from the flock—they're much easier to devour that way.

"Roller Coaster Christians" don't grow up spiritually; they just get older, and are always subject to the ups and downs of their circumstances and emotions!

Christian Growth Possibilities

Reprinted from *The Common Made Holy*, by Anderson, N. & Saucy, R., 1997, p, 363, Eugene, OR: Harvest Hours Publishers.

Conclusion: The onion skin vs. the banana skin principle.

We are not like bananas. God doesn't peel off the outside layer and we experience full freedom and maturity all at once. We are more like onions. Over time, God peels away layers of strongholds and lies we have believed and helps us experience more and more freedom and maturity as we grow.

The rest of this workbook contains several resources that we have put together to help you as you counsel/disciple people in your ministry.

- A master "Identity-Based Spiritual Formation" chart showing all three levels and their associated conflict and growth areas
- A sample discipleship plan for each maturity level, including one or two suggested lessons for each conflict/growth area. Each lesson also has suggested resources that are helpful for that conflict/growth area
- Resources to help guide and pray for struggling teenagers
- Helpful information on breaking bondage to sexual sin
- Information on gender confusion and how to help someone overcome it
- A section on seeking freedom from overt demonic involvement or abuse

We also have a series of videos that go along with Leader I and Leader II materials on our website. Visit our website and go to the bottom of the EPIC videos page. There is a link to the leader videos page. We are here to help you in any way; please let us know. Visit us at infusionnow.org or call us at 865-966-1153.

Master Conflict and Growth Chart

Area of Spiritual Formation	Level 1: Rooted In Christ Colossians 2:10	Level 2 Built up in Christ Colossians 2:7	Level 3 Walking in Christ Colossians 2:6
Spirit	**Conflict:** Lack of salvation or assurance *Ephesians 2:1-3*	**Conflict:** Walking according to the flesh *Galatians 5:19-21*	**Conflict:** Insensitive to the Spirit's leading *Hebrews 5:11-14*
	Growth: Child of God *1 John 3:1-3; 5:11-13*	**Growth:** Walking according to the Spirit *Galatians 5:22-23*	**Growth:** Led by the Spirit *Romans 8:14*
Mind	**Conflict:** Darkened understanding *Ephesians 4:18*	**Conflict:** Wrong beliefs or philosophy of life *Colossians 2:8*	**Conflict:** Pride *1 Corinthians 8:1*
	Growth: Renewed mind *Romans 12:2; Ephesians 4:23*	**Growth:** Rightly handling the word of truth *2 Timothy. 2:15*	**Growth:** Complete, equipped for every good work *2 Timothy 3:16-17*
Emotions	**Conflict:** Fear *Matthew 10:26-33*	**Conflict:** Anger *Ephesians 4:31* Anxiety *1 Peter 5:7* Depression *2 Corinthians 4*	**Conflict:** Discouragement Sorrow, Boredom *Galatians 6:9*
	Growth: Freedom *Galatians 5:1*	**Growth:** Joy, peace, patience *Galatians 5:22*	**Growth:** Contentment *Philippians 4:11*
Will	**Conflict:** Rebellion *1 Timothy 1:9 Matthew 16:24*	**Conflict:** Lack of self-control, Compulsiveness *1 Corinthians 3:1-3*	**Conflict:** Undisciplined *2 Thessalonians 3:7,11*
	Growth: Submission *Romans 13:1-2*	**Growth:** Self-control *Galatians 5:23*	**Growth:** Disciplined *1 Timothy 4:7-8*
Relationships	**Conflict:** Rejection *Ephesians 2:1-3*	**Conflict:** Unforgiveness *Colossians 3:1-3*	**Conflict:** Selfishness *Philippians 2:1-5 1 Corinthians 10:24*
	Growth: Acceptance *Romans 5:8; 15:7, 1 Peter 2:4*	**Growth:** Forgivness *Ephesians 4:32*	**Growth:** Brotherly love *Romans 12:10; Philippians 2:1-5*

Adapted from *Discipleship Counseling*, by Anderson, N., 2003, p. 123, Ventura, CA: Regal Books.

Discipleship Plan Primary Resources

These are the materials that are listed in the the following charts designed to help you with the identity based freedom counseling process.

All books/workbooks are available through Amazon or other book sellers

* Available also from Infusion Ministries (infusionnow.org or 865-966-1153)

*EPIC Materials:
Identity, Freedom, Journey, Leader I and Leader II

Stomping Out the Darkness - Neil Anderson & Dave Park
No matter what you see when you look in the mirror, God sees something better. That's because God sees you as the person you can become. Discover how to break free of negative thoughts and discover the joy of being a child of God.

Victory Over the Darkness - Neil Anderson
Neil T. Anderson and Dave Park give teens powerful guidance on Christ-centered living in today's pressure-cooker world. Youth will discover how to break the habits and bonds that lead to sin and rely on the Holy Spirit to avoid deception. Revealing the traps that will come their way, The Bondage Breaker® Youth Edition helps teens strip away superficiality and provides specific steps to achieving true freedom.

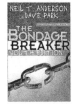

Bondage Breaker - Youth Edition - Neil Anderson & Dave Park
Neil T. Anderson and Dave Park give teens powerful guidance on Christ-centered living in today's pressure-cooker world. Youth will discover how to break the habits and bonds that lead to sin and rely on the Holy Spirit to avoid deception. Revealing the traps that will come their way, The Bondage Breaker® Youth Edition helps teens strip away superficiality and provides specific steps to achieving true freedom.

Bondage Breaker - Neil Anderson
Harmful habits, negative thinking, and irrational feelings can all lead to sinful behavior and keep you in bondage. If you feel trapped by any of these strongholds in your life, know that you are not alone—you can break free.

Discipleship Counseling

Building on the concepts found in Victory over the Darkness and The Bondage Breaker, Neil Anderson's counseling ministry guide provides clear information and excellent models to help you understand what discipleship counseling is all about. If you're a pastor, counselor, or lay leader, this resource will make you more comfortable, confident, and competent in your role as encourager. In turn, this will help you free people from their emotional pain and spiritual conflicts, as you guide them to a more complete understanding of who they are in Christ.

Freedom from Fear, Neil Anderson

Even believers can let the normal concerns of life get blown out of proportion, becoming ensnared in worry and anxiety: What if something happens to my spouse? What if something were to happen to one of my children? What if this plane crashes? Uncovering the surprising scope of fear in the body of Christ and how many Christians who believe in the Lord' s care and love are being kept from God' s best by their fears, Freedom from Fear shows readers how to take back their lives.

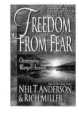

*Higher Ground

Sometimes we feel like we have to do the impossible when we are told to be like Jesus. Yet God knows we are not perfect and he still loves us. Higher Ground will help you explore deeper levels of faith that will strengthen your walk with Jesus. You will also learn how to make good decisions that will honor God and make every day count for him. Begin today and take the higher ground and live for Christ.

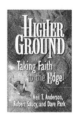

Who I Am in Christ Devotional

God never gives up on us. He remains steadfast in his desire to bless us, even when many of us are tempted to doubt his love. The great tragedy is that so many of us spend our lives trying to earn something we already have, the gift of life which God freely gives us when we decide to follow Christ. This amazing devotional from best selling author Neil Anderson will give readers back what the enemy is trying rob from them, an understanding of their special place in God's family. Here are 36 readings and prayers based on scriptural passages that assure us of God's love and our security and freedom in his kingdom

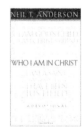

Discipleship Plan - Level 1: Rooted in Christ

	Conflict: Lack of salvation or assurance	Growth: I am a child of God
Spirit	**Lesson 1: Lack of salvation or assurance** HOW CAN I KNOW THAT I AM SAVED? Resources: • EPIC Identity, Message 2 & 3 • EPIC Identity Videos: "Your New Identity in Christ" and "Say Yes to the EPIC Life" • Stomping Out the Darkness, chapter 2 • Victory over the Darkness, chapter 2 **Lesson 2: Lies of the World** THE BIG LIE IS THAT MY NEEDS FOR ACCEPTANCE, SECURITY AND SIGNIFICANCE CAN BE MET BY THE WORLD, THE FLESH AND THE DEVIL. GOD ALONE MEETS MY DEEPEST NEEDS. Resources: • EPIC Identity, Message 2 • EPIC Identity Video: "False Identity Equations" • Stomping Out the Darkness, chapter 1 • Victory over the Darkness, chapter 1	**Lesson 1: I am a child of God** THE MOST IMPORTANT BELIEF ABOUT OURSELVES IS THIS: TO KNOW THE WE ARE HIS CHILDREN. Resources: • EPIC Identity, Message 2 • EPIC Identity Video: "Created in the Image of God" • Who I Am in Christ, chapter 2 **Lesson 2: I am a Saint** GOD IDENTIFIES ME AS A SAINT. WHAT DOES THIS MEAN AND HOW HAS THIS AFFECTED MY RELATIONSHIP TO SIN? Resources: • EPIC Identity, Message 2 • EPIC Identity Video: "Created in the Image of God" • Who I Am in Christ, chapter 8
	Conflict: Darkened Understanding	**Growth: Renewing the Mind**
Mind	**Lesson 1: Lost Knowledge of God** SIN HAS COST US A PERSONAL KNOWLEDGE OF GOD AND INTIMACY WITH HIM. Resources: • EPIC Identity, Message 2 • EPIC Identity Videos: "Your New Identity in Christ" • Stomping Out the Darkness, chapter 1 • Victory over the Darkness, chapter 1 **Lesson 2: Strongholds of the Mind** STRONGHOLDS ARE CAUSED BY CONTINUALLY OPENING DOORS TO THE ENEMY THROUGH DESTRUCTIVE THOUGHT PATTERNS AND HABITUAL SIN. Resources: • EPIC Identity Video: "Changing the Mind" • EPIC Freedom, Messages 2-3	**Lesson 1: Renewing the Mind** THE ROAD TO FREEDOM IS PAVED BY RENEWING OUR MINDS DAILY - REPLACING DESTRUCTIVE THOUGHT PATTERNS WITH TRUTH AND OVERCOMING OUR PAST. Resources: • EPIC Identity Video: "Changing the Mind" • EPIC Freedom, Message 2 • Bondage Breaker Youth Ed, chapter 4 • Bondage Breaker, chapter 4 **Lesson 2: Resisting Sin** WHAT IS REPENTANCE? HOW DO I REPENT? HOW DOES SUBMITTING TO GOD AND RESISTING THE DEVIL LEAD ME OUT OF BONDAGE TO LIES AND THE SIN THEY PRODUCE? Resources: • EPIC Freedom, Message 2 • EPIC Freedom Video: "Battle for the Mind"

Discipleship Plan - Level 1: Rooted in Christ, continued

	Conflict: Fear	Growth: Freedom
Emotions	**Lesson 1: What is Fear?** WE LIVE IN FEARFUL DAYS AND UNCERTAIN TIMES. WHERE DOES FEAR COME FROM AND HOW CAN I LIVE BY FAITH? Resources: • EPIC Identity Video: "Freed to Go" • EPIC Journey, Appendix - Overcoming Fear • Freedom from Fear, chapter 1 **Lesson 2: Fear of Failure** SUCCESSFUL PEOPLE FAIL. EVEN CELEBRATED BIBLICAL CHARACTERS FAILED. WHAT ARE THE KEYS TO OVERCOMING FEAR OF FAILURE? Resources: • EPIC Journey, Appendix - Overcoming Fear • Freedom from Fear, chapter 6	**Lesson 1: Dead to sin, Alive to Christ** HOW CAN A BELIEVER UNDERSTAND AND TAKE TO HEART THE TRUTH THAT THEY ARE NO LONGER ENSLAVED BY SIN? Resources: • EPIC Identity, Message 4 • EPIC Identity Videos: "Becoming Who You Really Are" • Stomping Out the Darkness, chapter 4 • Victory over the Darkness, chapter 4 **Lesson 2: Building a Strong Faith** BUILDING A STRONG FAITH BEGINS WITH KNOWING THE NATURE AND CHARACTER OF GOD. Resources: • EPIC Identity, Message 4 • EPIC Identity Video: "Knowing, Being, Doing" • Freedom from Fear, chapter 9
	Conflict: Rebelion	Growth: Submission
Will	**Lesson 1: Dealing with Rebellion** REBELLION IS A VERY SERIOUS ISSUE IN GOD'S SIGHT. HOW DOES REBELLION ORIGINATE IN MY SOUL AND HOW DO I OVERCOME IT? Resources: • EPIC Identity, Message 5 • EPIC Identity Video: "EPIC Love of the Father" • EPIC Journey, Petitions 3 & 6 • EPIC Journey Videos: "Seeking God's Guidance," "Yielding to God's Plans," & "Claiming Freedom from Sin & Bondage" • Stomping Out the Darkness, pg. 54-60 • Victory over the Darkness, pg. 91-98 **Lesson 2: Free to Live** I AM FREE TO EXPERIENCE ALL THAT GOD HAS PURPOSED FOR ME - A NEW LIFESTYLE FUELED BY NEW DESIRES. Resources: • EPIC Freedom, Message 2-3 • EPIC Freedom Videos: "Battle for the Mind," and "Breaking Down Strongholds"	**Lesson 1: Relating to Authority** TO GROW IN CHRIST I MUST LEARN HOW TO RELATE APPROPRIATELY TO THOSE IN AUTHORITY OVER ME. Resources: • EPIC Journey Petition 3 • EPIC Journey Video: "Seeking God's Guidance • Stomping Out the Darkness, chapter 8 • Victory over the Darkness, chapter 8 **Lesson 2: Overcoming Deception** DECEPTION OCCURS WHEN I DO NOT TAKE RESPONSIBILITY FOR MY CHRISTIAN GROWTH, LEAVING MYSELF OPEN TO THE LIES OF THE WORLD, THE FLESH AND THE DEVIL. Resources: • EPIC Freedom, Message 3 & 5 • EPIC Freedom Videos: "Breaking Down Strongholds" and "Living an EPIC Life" • EPIC Journey Petitions 1 & 8 • EPIC Journey Videos: "You Have an Abba Father" and "Asserting Your Victory in Christ" • Bondage Breaker Youth Edition chapter 11 • Bondage Breaker, chapter 11

Discipleship Plan - Level 1: Rooted in Christ, continued

	Conflict: Rejection	Growth: Acceptance

Relationships	**Lesson 1: Rejection**
	HOW DO I FIND HEALING FROM THE REJECTION I HAVE EXPERIENCED?
	
	Resources:
	• *EPIC Freedom, Message 4*
	• *EPIC Freedom Videos:*
	  "Forgiving from the Heart," and "Stories of Forgiveness"
	• *EPIC Journey, Petition 7*
	• *EPIC Journey Video:*
	  "Forgiving Those Who Hurt You"
	• *Stomping Out the Darkness, chapter 12*
	• *Victory over the Darkness, chapter 12*
	
	Lesson 2: Fear of Man
	HOW DO I OVERCOME A FEAR OF MAN AND EXPERIENCE TRUE FREEDOM?
	
	Resources:
	• *EPIC Freedom, Message 3*
	• *EPIC Freedom Video:*
	  "Breaking Down Strongholds"
	• *EPIC Journey Appendix -*
	  Overcoming Fear
	• *Freedom from Fear, chapter 4*
		Lesson 1: I Am Accepted
		HOW DO I KNOW THAT I AM FULLY ACCEPTED BY GOD? WHAT LIES PREVENT ME FROM SEEING MYSELF AS CHRIST SEES ME?
		
		Resources:
		• *EPIC Identity Videos:*
		  "Your New Identity in Christ" and
		  "Becoming Who You Really Are"
		• *Who I Am in Christ, chapter 1*
		
		Lesson 2: I Belong to God
		BELONGING TO GOD AND BEING A PART OF GOD'S KINGDOM BRINGS PURPOSE AND MEANING TO MY LIFE.
		
		Resources:
		• *EPIC Identity, Message 2*
		• *EPIC Identity Video:*
		  "Your New Identity in Christ"
		• *EPIC Identity, Message 4*
		• *EPIC Identity Video:*
		  "Becoming Who You Really Are"
		• *Stomping Out the Darkness, chapters 1-3*
		• *Who I am in Christ, chapter. 6-7*

Discipleship Plan - Level 2: Built up in Christ

	Conflict: Walking in to the Flesh	Growth: Walking in the Spirit
Spirit	**Lesson 1: Walking According to the Flesh** WHAT ARE THE FLESHLY HABITS THAT KEEP ME FROM WALKING IN THE SPIRIT? Resources: • *EPIC Freedom, Messages 2-3* • *EPIC Freedom Videos: "Battle for the Mind," and "Breaking Down Strongholds"* • *EPIC Journey Video: "Claiming Freedom from Sin & Bondage"* • *Stomping Out the Darkness, pg. 58-60;* • *Victory Over Darkness, chapter 5* • *Higher Ground, Chapter 8* **Lesson 2: Shackles of Condemnation** HOW DO I BREAK THE SHACKLES OF CONDEMNATION THROUGH CONFESSION OF SIN? Resources: • *EPIC Journey, Petition 6* • *EPIC Journey Video: "Claiming Freedom from Sin & Bondage*	**Lesson 1: Walking by to the Spirit** CAN I REALLY WALK IN THE SPIRIT WHEN I AM SURROUNDED BY THE WORLD, THE FLESH, AND THE DEVIL? HOW DO I WALK IN THE SPIRIT AND RECOGNIZE THE FRUIT OF THE SPIRIT IN MY LIFE? Resources: • *Stomping Out the Darkness p. 60-65;* • *Victory Over the Darkness, p. 99-106* **Lesson 2: Free from Sin** AM I REALLY FREE FROM THE POWER OF SIN AND ITS ABILITY TO CONTROL MY LIFE? Resources: • *EPIC Journey, Petitions 6 & 8* • *EPIC Journey Video: "Claiming Freedom from Sin & Bondage"*
	Conflict: Wrong belief system	**Growth: Believing God's word**
Mind	**Lesson 1: Temptations** WHAT LEADS TO TEMPTATION AND CAN I REALLY SAY "NO" TO TEMPTATION? HOW CAN I OVERCOME THE TEMPTATION TO SIN? Resources: • *EPIC Freedom, Message 2* • *EPIC Freedom Videos: "Battle for the Mind," and "Examples of Battle for the Mind."* • *Stomping Out the Darkness, p. 98-100* • *Victory Over the Darkness, p.154-158* • *Bondage Breaker Youth Ed., chapter 9* • *Bondage Breaker Adult Ed, chapter 9* **Lesson 2: Wrong Belief = Wrong Living** HAVING A WRONG BELIEF SYSTEM ABOUT MYSELF AND GOD WILL RESULT IN WRONG CHOICES AND WRONG LIVING. Resources: • *EPIC Freedom, Message 1* • *EPIC Freedom Videos: "EPIC Walk of Faith" and "Evidence of Faith."* • *Stomping Out the Darkness, chapter 6* • *Victory Over the Darkness chapter 6*	**Lesson 1: Repentance** BELIEVERS ARE CALLED TO A LIFESTYLE OF REPENTANCE. WHAT IS REPENTANCE, WHY IS IT SO IMPORTANT, AND WHAT IS INVOLVED IN BIBLICAL REPENTANCE? Resources: • *EPIC Journey, Message 2* • *EPIC Journey Video: "The Proper Worship of God" (Parts 1&2)* • *Discipleship Counseling pg. 125-128* **Lesson 2: Rightly handling the word of truth** HOW CAN I KNOW THE BIBLE AND THE GOD OF THE BIBLE ARE TRUSTWORTHY OBJECTS OF MY FAITH? Resources: • *EPIC Freedom, Message 1* • *EPIC Freedom Video: "EPIC Walk of Faith."* • *Stomping Out the Darkness, chapter 8* • *Victory Over the Darkness, chapter 8*

Discipleship Plan - Level 2: Built up in Christ, continued

	Conflict: Anger	Growth: Joy, Peace, Patience
Emotions	**Lesson 1: Anger** WHAT CAUSES ANGER AND HOW DOES IT GROW INTO A STRONGHOLD? HOW DO I BREAK DOWN THIS STRONGHOLD? Resources: • *EPIC Freedom, Message 3* • *EPIC Freedom Video-"Breaking Down Strongholds."* • *Stomping Out the Darkness, chapter 7* • *Victory Over the Darkness, chapter 7* **Lesson 2: Fear of Death** THE FEAR OF DEATH UNDERMINES THE BELIEVER'S EXPERIENCE OF LIFE HERE AND NOW. HOW DO I OVERCOME THIS FEAR? Resources: • *EPIC Journey, Petition 9* • *EPIC Journey Video: "Claiming Your Protection."* • *Freedom from Fear, chapter 5*	**Lesson 1: Overcoming Anxiety** WHAT IS ANXIETY, AND HOW CAN BELIEVERS LIVE IN PEACE? Resources: • *EPIC Journey, Petition 1* • *EPIC Journey Video: "You Have an Abba Father;"* • *Stomping Out the Darkness, chapter 7* • *Discipleship Counseling, pg. 55* • *Freedom from Fear, chapter 2 & 7* **Lesson 2: Overcoming Depression** DEPRESSION IS THE "COMMON COLD" OF MENTAL/ EMOTIONAL AFFLICTIONS. WHAT IS DEPRESSION, AND WHAT ARE THE SIGNS OF DEPRESSION? WHAT LIES FUEL DEPRESSION, AND WHAT STEPS CAN I TAKE TO RESTORE JOY? Resources: • *EPIC Freedom, Message 1* • *EPIC Freedom Videos:-"Evidence of Faith,"* • *EPIC Journey, Petition 3* • *EPIC Journey Video -"Seeking God's Guidance."* • *Stomping Out the Darkness, chapter 7* • *Victory Over the Darkness, chapter 7*
	Conflict: Lack of Self-Control	Growth: Self-Control
Will	**Lesson 1: Dealing with Abuse & Trusting People** HOW DO I HANDLE AN AUTHORITY FIGURE WHO IS ABUSIVE, AND HOW DO I TEAR DOWN THE LIES AND REMOVE THE BITTERNESS CAUSED BY ABUSE? Resources: • *EPIC Freedom, Message 4* • *EPIC Freedom Video: "Forgiving from the Heart."* • *Stomping Out the Darkness, chapter 7-8* • *Victory Over the Darkness, chapter 7-8* • *Discipleship Counseling, pg. 278-90* **Lesson 2: Satan's Stealthy Lies** SATAN CAN INFLUENCE ME BY PLACING THOUGHTS IN MY MIND, EVEN THOUGH I AM A BELIEVER. HOW DO I RECOGNIZED THESE THOUGHTS AND TAKE THEM CAPTIVE? Resources: • *EPIC Freedom, Message 4* • *EPIC Freedom Videos:-"Battle for the Mind," and "Examples of Battle for the Mind*	**Lesson 1: Stand, Stand, Stand** IN EPHESIANS 6:10-17 WE ARE CALLED TO STAND FIRM WHEN ATTACKED BY SATAN. HOW CAN I STAND STRONG IN THE FACE OF THE ENEMY? Resources: • *EPIC Freedom, Message 2* • *EPIC Freedom Video: "Battle for the Mind."*

Discipleship Plan - Level 2: Built up in Christ, continued

	Conflict: Unforgiveness	Growth: Forgiveness
Relationships	**Lesson 1: Being Real with Yourself** MY EMOTIONS ARE REAL, AND HIDING, BURYING, OR BEING RULED BY MY FEELINGS WILL ONLY MAKE MATTERS WORSE. HOW SHOULD I RESPOND TO MY EMOTIONS? Resources: • *Stomping Out the Darkness, chapter10* • *Victory Over the Darkness, chapter 10* **Lesson 2: Bitterness** HOW DO I DEAL WITH BITTERNESS IN A BIBLICAL WAY THAT RESTORES AND PROTECTS BOTH MY HEART AND MY RELATIONSHIPS? Resources: • *EPIC Freedom, Message 4* • *EPIC Freedom Videos: "Forgiving from the Heart" and "Stories of Forgiveness.* • *Discipleship Counseling, chapter 11*	**Lesson 1: Forgiveness from the Heart** BITTERNESS IS RAMPANT IN THIS WORLD AND EVEN IN THE CHURCH. HOW CAN I LEAD MYSELF AND OTHERS TO FORGIVE AND TEAR OUT ALL BITTERNESS? Resources: • *EPIC Journey, Petition 7;* • *Discipleship Counseling, chapter 11* • *Stomping Out the Darkness, chapter 11* • *Victory Over the Darkness, chapter 11* **Lesson 2: I am Forgiven and Complete in Christ** HOW IS BEING FORGIVEN THE FOUNDATION OF MY COMPLETENESS IN CHRIST? Resources: • *Who I Am in Christ, chapters 11-12* • *Stomping Out the Darkness, chapters 1-3*

Discipleship Plan - Level 3: Walking in Christ

	Conflict: Insensitive to Spirit's Leading	Growth: Led by the Spirit
Spiritual	**Lesson 1: Living Out Your Faith** HOW DO I FUNCTION AS A CHILD OF GOD IN MY HOME, CHURCH, AND RELATIONSHIPS? Resources: • *EPIC Freedom, Message 5* • *EPIC Journey Video: "Living an EPIC Life"* • *EPIC Leader II, Message 3* • *Ephesians 1* **Lesson 2: When Heaven is Silent** WHAT HAPPENS WHEN GOD SEEMS SILENT? HOW DO I CONTINUE TO FOLLOW THE SPIRIT'S LEADING? Resource: • *Higher Ground, chapter 10*	**Lesson 1: Led by the Spirit** AM I BEING LED BY THE HOLY SPIRIT? WHAT DOES THE SPIRIT LED WALK LOOK LIKE? Resources: • *Stomping Out the Darkness, p.62-65* • *Higher Ground, chapter 6* **Lesson 2: Understand and Helping the Disciple** HOW DO I COUNSEL THE SPIRITUALLY OPPRESSED AND HELP LEAD THEM OUT FROM DEMONIC INFLUENCE AND INTO FREEDOM? Resources: • *EPIC Leader 1, Message 3* • *Discipleship Counseling, chapter 7*
	Conflict: Pride	**Growth: Adequate, Equipped**
Mind	**Lesson 1: Pride** HOW DO I UNMASK PRIDE IN MY LIFE, OVERCOME IT, AND WALK IN TRUE HUMILITY? Resources: • *EPIC Journey, Petition 8* • *EPIC Journey Video: "Asserting your Victory in Christ"* • *Discipleship Counseling, chapter 13* **Lesson 2: Doubting God** WRONG LIVING OFTEN STEMS FROM DOUBT. WHAT IS DOUBT, AND HOW DO I CROSS OVER INTO LIVING BY FAITH? Resources: • *EPIC Freedom, Message 1* • *EPIC Freedom Video: "EPIC Walk of Faith"*	**Lesson 1: The Sanctification Process** WHAT ARE THE SPIRITUAL CONFLICTS AND AVENUES FOR GROWTH AT EACH STAGE OF THE SANCTIFYING PROCESS? Resources: • *EPIC Freedom Video: "A Call to Ministry"* • *Discipleship Counseling, chapter 5*

Discipleship Plan - Level 3: Walking in Christ, continued

	Conflict: Discouragement and Sorrow	Growth: Contentment
Emotions	**Lesson 1: Cost of Discipleship** OFTEN WE SAY, "IS THIS IT?" "HOW CAN I GROW MORE IN MY FAITH?" GOD HAS MORE FOR ALL OF US, BUT WE MUST EMBRACE THE COST OF DISCIPLESHIP. Resources: • *EPIC Freedom, message 1* • *EPIC Freedom Videos: "Evidences of Faith," and "A Call to Ministry"* • *Higher Ground, chapter 10* **Lesson 2: Fear of the Lord** WHAT IS THE ONE FEAR I MUST EMBRACE THAT WILL SHATTER ALL OTHER FEARS I ENCOUNTER Resource: • *Freedom from Fear, chapter 11*	**Lesson 1: Building a Strong Faith** BUILDING A STRONG FAITH BEGINS WITH KNOWING THE NATURE AND CHARACTER OF GOD. Resources: • *EPIC Journey, Petition 1* • *EPIC Journey Videos: "You Have an Abba Father."* • *Freedom from Fear, chapter 9*
	Conflict: Undisciplined	**Growth: Disciplined**
Will	**Lesson 1: Living a Lifestyle of Freedom** HOW CAN I STAY FREE AND DISCIPLINED SURROUNDED BY A CULTURE OF UNDISCIPLINED LIFESTYLES? Resources: • *EPIC Freedom, Message 5* • *EPIC Freedom Video: "A Call to Ministry."* **Lesson 2: Free to Live** NOT ONLY AM I FREE FROM SLAVERY TO SIN, BUT I AM FREE TO LIVE FOR THE KINGDOM OF GOD. Resources: • *EPIC Freedom, Message 5* • *EPIC Freedom Video: "Living an EPIC Life."*	**Lesson 1: The Life and Character of the Discipler** WHAT IS THE CHARACTER OF AN EFFECTIVE CHRISTIAN LEADER? WHAT QUALITIES MUST I NURTURE TO LEAD OTHERS INTO FREEDOM AND SPIRITUAL MATURITY? Resources: • *EPIC Leader - Message 3: "The Life and Character of the Discipler"* **Lesson 2: Leading Someone through EPIC Journey** HOW CAN I N LEAD OTHERS OUT OF SPIRITUAL BONDAGE THROUGH THE LORD'S PRAYER JOURNEY? Resources: • *EPIC Leader I workbook - Session 7* • *EPIC Journey Workbook* • *EPIC Journey Videos*

Discipleship Plan - Level 3: Walking in Christ, continued		
	Conflict: Selfishness	**Growth: Brotherly Love**
Relationships	**Lesson 1: Give Your Life Away to Others** THE GREATEST ACT OF LOVE IS TO GIVE YOUR LIFE TO OTHERS AS JESUS DID. THIS IS THE MARK OF A TRUE LEADER. Resources: • *EPIC Freedom, Message 5* • *EPIC Freedom Video: "A Call to Ministry* • *Stomping Out the Darkness, chapter 8* • *Victory Over the Darkness, chapter 8* **Lesson 2: Walk in Christ** MY WALK WITH CHRIST IS A DAILY JOURNEY OF CELEBRATING GOD'S CHARACTER AND WORKS, AFFIRMING MY IDENTITY IN HIM, TRUSTING IN HIS PROMISES, AND MAKING DECISIONS ON THE BASIS THESE REALITIES. Resources: • *EPIC Identity, message 2* • *Ephesians 4-6* • *EPIC Identity Video: "Knowing, Doing, Being."*	**Lesson 1: Called to Minister** I AM CALLED TO MAKE DISCIPLES, AND HELP BELIEVERS WALK IN FREEDOM! Resources: • *EPIC Freedom, Message 5* • *EPIC Freedom Video: "A Call to Ministry."* • *Higher Ground, chapter 7*

Other Helpful Resources

All books/workbooks are available through Amazon or other book sellers

* Available also from Infusion Ministries (infusionnow.org or 865-966-1153)

Breaking Through to Spiritual Maturity - Neil Anderson

A 13- to 26-week reproducible study course that will enable pastors, study leaders and counselors to lead those who seek to grow into spiritual maturity as they take possession of the victory Christ freely offers. Participants will learn that Christ gives every believer a new identity and victory over sin and also how to recognize and overcome spiritual deception and to exercise the authority God gives all believers. Provides specific steps to claiming freedom in Christ. The flexible format allows the lessons to be presented in 60- or 90-minute sessions with additional flexibility in the number (13-26) of sessions to be presented. This material enables any group leader or teacher to lead this study who is sincerely and prayerfully following Christ.

*Busting Free

Busting Free is a dynamic youth group study based on the best selling books Stomping Out the Darkness and The Bondage Breaker Youth Edition. The 13 sessions cover how to recognize and overcome spiritual deception, how to claim the authority God gives to all believers, and what steps to take for claiming freedom in Christ! This study includes reproducible student pages, a spiritual health survey, The Steps to Freedom in Christ designed for teens, and much more.

*Free (devotional)
Free takes you on an amazing journey to the ultimate source of wisdom and power for living your faith 24/7. Packed with great stories and life-changing ideas, this inspiring book helps challenge you to connect with a God who really loves you. In quick daily readings, you'll discover:
- God loves you, even though you're not perfect
- How to win over temptations
- Key promises to help you survive, and even triumph, in hard times

This 40-day devotional will help you understand the power of real-life Christianity and how Jesus gives you everything you need to overcome temptation and live for him. By living for Jesus 24/7, you will experience a life of true freedom that's better than you ever thought possible.

*Men of the Banner

Jesus promised us that the Truth would set us free. Yet, so many men in our churches are hurting and struggling with condemning thoughts, compulsive behavior, despair, and spiritual bondage. We are called to reach out to one another with a message of identity and freedom that brings true healing. Join Jimmy Taylor, author of the Men of the Banner Bible Study, as he shares about his own struggles and failures and how he found freedom.

Overcoming Addictive Behavior

For I have the desire to do what is good, but I cannot carry it out. For I do not do the good I want to do, but the evil I do not want to do—this I keep on doing. (Romans 7:18-19 NIV). Addiction forges its own chains of pain and problems that grow with each day and seem impossible to overcome. If you are, or someone you know is, a captive of addictive behavior, Neil Anderson and Mike Quarles have both a message of hope and a plan of action. Anyone can be set free from addictive behavior, can experience victory in Jesus, and can become an overcomer in life! The key is to identify the root cause of your problem and, instead of running away from it, run to God! Do this, and your mind and spirit will be renewed; and no matter what you struggle with, you will find your freedom in Christ!

Overcoming Negative Self-Image

Knowing who you are in Christ is your key to victory in life. Do you often wonder what God thinks of you or whether he thinks of you at all? Do you have a negative self-image--a low opinion of yourself and life in general--that you would love to overcome? You can do it! You can turn your life around and never look back. The one and only key is to understand who God wants you to be. That's the heart of Neil Anderson's breakthrough freedom-in-Christ message. Every last one of us--no matter how much we suffer from low self-esteem, insecurity, or abusive behavior-- can be free from our pain and problems, experience victory in Jesus, and become an overcomer in life!

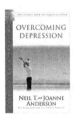

Overcoming Depression

Overcoming Depression can provide healing and freedom for millions of Christians who suffer silently from depression. This Christ-centered road map to recovery balances spiritual and physical symptoms, leading those with depression, and those in the church who must help them, to both a thorough understanding and a comprehensive treatment. Now is the time to get Overcoming Depression into the hands of Christians everywhere, helping those who are desperately in need of its powerful and life-changing message.

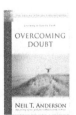

Overcoming Doubt

Everyone has doubts. Doubting is a normal part of the process of arriving at an ultimate decision of belief or unbelief. Persistent doubting, however can affect your mental health, keeping you from living a productive life. The answer is to be assured of what you believe and start living by faith in God. Dr. Anderson explains the nature of doubting and the nature of faith, leading you to go beyond your doubts to live a fruitful live. You will come to understand the spiritual battle waged daily for your mind, as it is here where many doubts are formed. You are God's dear child and he has promised to guide you into truth. Remember that God is truth and he cannot lie and learn to overcome your doubts by choosing to believe in him and his timeless Word.

Purity Under Pressure

In this book, you'll find out the difference between being friends, dating, and having a relationship. You'll see how the physical stuff fits in. And you'll get answers to the questions you're asking:

What is real love?
How can you keep a good relationship from going bad?
What does God say about sex?
How far is too far?
What if you're trapped?
Can you ever be free? Can you ever "start over"?
Yes. You can be free...in Christ. No hype. No big lectures. Just straightforward talk to help you figure out what to do when your purity's under pressure.

Setting your Church Free

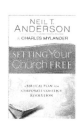

Corporate sin robs the spiritual vitality and fruitfulness of churches, keeping them from being free in Christ. In Setting Your Church Free trusted authors Neil T. Anderson and Charles Mylander offer practical and life-giving tools for dealing biblically with corporate sin in the church. Offering a balanced approach, this unique book takes into account the reality of the spiritual world as well as the need for correcting leadership and administration problems.

Wining the Battle Within

For too many believers, God's wonderful creation of sex has become a source of spiritual slavery rather than a liberating blessing. Neil T. Anderson presents a clarifying, refreshing look at God's plan for sex and how Christians can release a distorted view of physical intimacy and embrace a pure, godly view of this gift. With biblical advice and compassion, Anderson points to the way out of confusion and shame by

• exposing the guilt, anger, and fear involved in sexual struggles

• showing how believing the truth breaks the sexual and emotional lies

• giving practical steps to overcome spiritual entrapment with God's Word

As Christians grasp what the Bible says about who they really are—God's loved children and new creations in his Son—they will be able to enjoy and value his marvelous design for their emotions and bodies.

*My Identity in Christ Cards

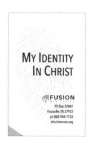

This handy tri-fold card fits into your wallet or purse and is full of truth declarations and supporting scriptures to remind you that in Christ you are accepted, secure significant, and successful. For larger bulk orders please contact us.

Special Cases

Prayers for Struggling Teenagers

Rescuing the rebellious teen

There is no question that our teens live in a rebellious generation. As a young person goes through the "Steps to Freedom" or the "EPIC Journey" and examines each area where he/she may have acted in rebellion, submission to authority will become more natural. But in more difficult cases, such as continuing abuse in the home, further counseling may be needed. You may have to direct them back to the forgiveness step if there is no resolution in the area of rebellion.

Pray a hedge of protection around the rebellious teen. If a young person is unwilling to go through the "Steps to Freedom" or the "EPIC Journey," we must pray! First, that God would place his holy angels around the teenager, and that his mind would be his own, a quiet place for him and God. Then, that God would convict him of his rebellion and draw him to repentance.

Praying a hedge of protection

In our struggle against evil, we are dealing with spiritual powers. Therefore, we must put on the whole armor of God and stand against the attacks of the wicked one. "For the weapons of our warfare are not of the flesh, but divinely powerful for the destruction of strongholds" (2 Corinthians 10:4).

God placed a hedge around Job, and Satan complained about its effectiveness against him: "Hast not thou made a hedge about him, and about his house, and about all that he hath on every side..." (Job 1:10)

There are three parts to the prayer for a hedge of protection:

First, ask God to bind the power of Satan in the life of your family. Be mighty, through God, to pull down strongholds, "no man can enter into a strong man's house, and spoil his goods, except he will first bind the strong man..." (Mark 3:27).

Second, pray in the name and through the blood of the Lord Jesus Christ. "And whatsoever you shall ask in My name, that will I do, that the Father may be glorified in the Son" (John 14:13). Christ's name is Protector, the Good Shepherd that gives his life for his sheep.

Third, claim the Scripture that relates to the kind of protection that is needed. For example, protection from sin, "For sin shall not have dominion over you..." Romans 6:14); protection from discouragement, "...I will never leave you, nor forsake you" (Hebrew 13:5); protection from rebellion...(I Samuel 15:23).

Heavenly Father, I ask you in the name and through the blood of the Lord Jesus Christ to bind and rebuke Satan, and to put a hedge of protection around me and each one in my family. *"And I am sure of this, that he who began a good work in you will bring it to completion at the day of Jesus Christ."* (Philippians 1:6). I ask you to draw (name) to confess and renounce the rebellion so that he/she might walk free in Christ. In the Name of Jesus, our Shepherd, Amen.

Prayer for a rebellious teen (fill in the name in the blanks):

Loving Heavenly Father, in the name of our Lord Jesus Christ, I bring before you (_____). I ask for the Holy Spirit's guidance that I might pray in the Spirit. I thank you, Heavenly Father, that you have sovereign control. I thank you for the qualities and Christ-likeness which I see that you have placed in (_____). In the name of the Lord Jesus Christ and as a priest of God, I ask for mercy and forgiveness for the sins of (_____) which have grieved you. I plead the sufficiency of the blood of Christ to meet the full penalty his/her sins deserve. I claim back the ground of his/he life, which he/she has given to Satan by believing the enemy's lies. In the name of the Lord Jesus Christ, I resist all of Satan's activity to hold (_____) in blindness and darkness. Exercising my authority, which is given to me in my union with the Lord Jesus Christ, I pull down the strongholds which the kingdom of darkness has formed against (_____). I smash and break and destroy all those plans formed against (_____) 's mind, his/her will, his/her emotions, and body. I destroy in prayer the spiritual blindness and deafness that Satan keeps upon him/her. I invite the Holy Spirit of God to bring the fullness of his power to convict, to bring to repentance, and to lead (_____) to freedom in the Lord Jesus Christ. I cover him/her with the blood of the Lord Jesus Christ, and I break Satan's power to blind him/her to the truth of God. Believing that your Holy Spirit is leading me, I claim (_____) for you in the name of the Lord Jesus Christ, and I thank you for the answer to my prayer. In the name of the Lord Jesus Christ, I joyfully lay this prayer before you in the worthiness of his completed work. Amen.

Prayer for a rebellious son/daughter:

I bow humbly before the Heavenly Father to intercede for my son/daughter, (_____). I bring him/her before you in the name of the Lord Jesus Christ. I thank you that you have loved (_____) with the love of Calvary. I thank you that you gave him/her to us to love and nurture in Christ. I ask you to forgive us for all of our failures to guide him/her in the way he/she ought to go. I am thankful that you are sovereign and can use even the depths of sin to which he/she is now enslaved to rebound to your glory. I praise you for this great trial that humbles my heart before you.

Accepting my position of being "mighty through God to the pulling down of strongholds," I bring all of the works of the Lord Jesus Christ to focus directly against the powers of darkness that blind and bind (_____). I pray the victory of our Lord's incarnation, crucifixion, resurrection, ascension, and glorification directly against all of Satan's power in (_____) 's life. I bind up all forces of darkness set to destroy him/her. And I loose him/her from their blinding in the name of the Lord Jesus Christ. I invite the Holy Spirit to move upon (_____) 's heart and to convict him/her of sin, unrighteousness, and the judgment to come. In my priestly ministry, I confess (_____) 's sins unto you and plead your compassionate mercy toward him/her. I confess his/her yielding to all manner of fleshly sins, which has given Satan a place in his/her life. I plead the blood of Christ over his/her wickedness and wait upon the Holy Spirit to bring him/her to repentance, faith, and life in the Lord Jesus Christ. By faith, I claim (_____) for a life yielded to serve the true and living God in the name of the Lord Jesus Christ. Amen.

Prayer for a child going through trials:

Loving Heavenly Father, I bring my daughter/son (_____) to your throne in prayer. Through the person and work of the Lord Jesus Christ, I present (_____) to you as one made perfect and acceptable unto you. May the blessed Holy Spirit guide me during this time of prayer and enable me to pray in the Spirit. I bring all powers of darkness seeking to assault and afflict (_____) to account before the true and living God. I pray for (_____) union with the mighty victory of the Lord Jesus Christ against these powers. All powers of darkness seeking to hurt my daughter's/son's mind, body or soul, I bind up in the name of the Lord Jesus Christ. I loose (_____) from their attack and plead over her/him the precious blood of the Lord Jesus Christ. As (_____) parent and a priest of God, I claim my place of full authority over all powers of darkness. In your grace, we receive this experience as being significant in the sovereign purposes of God. Teach (_____) and our family through this trial. In the name of the Lord Jesus Christ. Amen.

Breaking a Bondage to Sexual Sin

If a person is not experiencing freedom from some type of sexual sin after going through the "Steps Freedom" or "EPIC Journey", it could be that he/she has failed to deal specifically with all of the uses of his/her body as an instrument of unrighteousness. People may often find help by obeying James 5:16, which says to *"... confess your sins to one another and pray for one another, that you may be healed. The prayer of a righteous person has great power as it is working."* Take care that they do not share their problems with just anyone, but help them seek out trusted Christ-following leaders. Relationships that are not God-honoring may need to be broken off. Sexually explicit materials must be destroyed. Cable/satellite channels, or even internet connections might need to be disconnected, or freedom will quickly give way to bondage once again.

Overcoming Gender Confusion

Gender dysphoria (confusion) is a conflict between a person's biological sex and his/her self-perceived gender identity. In recent years, the issues surrounding gender confusion and transgenderism have emerged from the shadows and into the mainstream of modern society. Today, it is heralded as "evidence" that gender is a state of mind divorced from biological sex and can even be changed.

The word of God makes clear that the Creator has permanently assigned each person's gender at birth, in harmony with his/her biological sex (see Genesis 1:26, Mark 10:6-9). However, after the fall, every aspect of the human condition fell under the destructive effect of sin. Gender confusion is one manifestation of sin's impact upon the human mind and body.

How do we minister to believers who are under the power of this spiritual stronghold, and help them to walk in freedom as the man or woman God has made them to be? In a general sense, we should treat this stronghold as we would any other – as a battle for the mind. In this battle, victory is won by placing God's voice above all competing voices and emotions; by renouncing lies and internalizing truths; by opening oneself up to the transforming work of the Holy Spirit.

To minister specifically to someone struggling with gender identity, here is an outline to one approach that is presented in greater detail in the EPIC Journey workbook:

1. Receive Christ as your Savior (John 3:16, John 14:6, Romans 6:23, Matthew 11:28-30). Receive and affirm the truth that your salvation is secure in him (1 John 5:11-13). Salvation entails not only a change in destination (heaven to hell), but a change in identity (sinner to saint) and Spirit empowered transformation into the likeness of Christ (2 Corinthians 3:17-18).

2. Receive and affirm Jesus as the Creator, who has the right to identify and define all that he has created (Colossians 1:16, John 1:1-3). Repent of and renounce any false "gods" or false identity equations which may feed into gender confusion (EPIC Journey, Chapter 2).

3. Receive and affirm Jesus as the High Priest who has been tempted in every way we are - even with gender confusion (Hebrews 4:15-16)! His identification with us, his perfect obedience to the Father in the midst of temptation, and his substitutionary death upon the cross are the basis for our salvation and deliverance from slavery to sin. Repent of and renounce the lie that God does not understand your pain and has provided no way out of the temptations associated with gender confusion
(1 Corinthians 10:13).

4. Receive and affirm that Jesus truly loves you, is trustworthy, and has your best interests at heart (Romans 5:7-8, Jeremiah 29:11). Because he loved you by dying for you when you were a sinner, you can trust him to love you permanently and unconditionally, now that you are his child. You can trust him to lead you in a way that results in his glory and your highest good. Renounce the lie that you will only experience fullness of life by attempting to live as a person of the opposite gender.

5. Receive and affirm that God and his word are supreme (Isaiah 55:8-9, 2 Timothy 3:16-17, Proverbs 3:5-6). Human feelings about gender (or anything else) do not dictate what is true – God and his word dictate what is true. Agree with Jesus who prayed to the Father in John 17:17, "Your word is truth." Renounce any human or spiritual voices competing with God's voice in this matter of gender identity.

6. Repent of lies you have believed about your gender identity. Repent of any steps you have taken, or considered taking, to identify, behave and present yourself as a member of the opposite sex (Deuteronomy 22:5, 1 Corinthians 6:19-20). Receive his forgiveness (1 John 1:9). Agree with God and proclaim who you truly are in Christ, including your God-given gender (EPIC Identity, Message 4, pp 32-34).

7. Forgive any who have abused or mistreated you in any way that may have opened doors to lies about your gender (EPIC Journey, Chapter 7). Include those who have influenced you toward transgenderism in attempts to alleviate your gender confusion. The road to freedom is paved with forgiveness!

8. Maintain your freedom by praying the 5 Rs (EPIC Freedom, Message 3):
   - Ask the Spirit to **reveal** the things you need to repent of
   - **Repent** by confessing the sin or lie God has revealed and receive his forgiveness
   - **Renounce** the sin and the lie behind the sin
   - **Renew** your mind with God's word.
   - **Resist** the enemy

9. Maintain your freedom by praying for and entering into relationships with believers who will love you just as you are and who will faithfully pray for you and point you toward your true identity and freedom in Christ.

In the case of gender confusion, many more factors may be at play, so utilize the EPIC Journey workbook and video series (infusionnow.org – EPIC Videos). These resources provide a framework for comprehensively working through spiritual conflicts, and breaking down spiritual strongholds.

Seeking Freedom from Satanic Ritual Abuse (SRA)

In SRA, Satanists do everything in direct opposition to Christianity. Satanism is the antithesis of Christianity. Satan is anti-Christ. The importance of renunciation—If a person is recalling SRA events, have them renounce any possible involvement from the chart below and then announce their new life in Christ reality.

Kingdom of Darkness	Kingdom of Light
I renounce ever signing my name over to Satan or having my name signed over to Satan.	I announce that my name is now written in the lamb's Book of Life.
I renounce any ceremony where I may have been married to Satan.	I announce that I am the bride of Christ.
I renounce any and all covenants or agreements, promises with Satan.	I announce that I have a new covenant with Christ.
I renounce any sacrifices that were made for me where Satan would claim ownership of me.	I announce that I belong to God because of the sacrifice that Jesus Christ made for me on the cross.
I renounce all Satanic assignments for my life including duties, marriage and children.	I announce and commit myself to know and do only the will of God and accept only his guidance.
I renounce all spirit guides assigned to me.	I announce and accept only the leading of the Holy Spirit.
I renounce giving my blood in a satanic ritual.	I trust only on the blood of the Lord Jesus for my salvation.
I renounce ever eating flesh or drinking book for satanic worship.	By faith I eat only the flesh and drink only the blood of Jesus in Holy Communion
I renounce every sacrifice made on my behalf by Satanists, whereby my worship is claimed for Satan.	I announce that Christ is my sacrifice and I belong to him because I have been bought and purchased by the blood of the Lamb, and I worship him only.
I renounce all guardians and Satanic parents that were assigned to me.	I announce that God is my Heavenly Father and the Holy Spirit is my guardian by which I am sealed.
I renounce any ceremony where I was assigned to be a high priest/priestess for satanic service	I announce that in Christ I am a member of a chosen race, a royal priesthood, and a holy nation. I am a person for God's own possession. I serve him alone.

The importance of renouncing specific events and memories

For SRA victims, the renunciations on the previous page are an expansion of the confession made by the early church, "I renounce Satan and all his works and ways."

The renunciations are generic since all SRA victims have been subjected, in one form or another, to these unholy bonds through satanic rituals. As the Holy Spirit reveals the specific things hidden in darkness, they must be specifically renounced. We always take each victim through the "Steps to Freedom" or "The Lord's Prayer Journey" (EPIC Journey) first since that will resolve much of their bondage. Then, more specific assignments and experiences can be resolved as God be reveals them.

Symptoms of Ritual Abuse

One sign of SRA is affectlessness (lack of emotion). Another is blocked memories, a condition where people simply cannot recall any events or happenings related to specific periods of time in their lives.

Affectlessness is the result of programming. For example, victims may be conditioned to believe that if they cry, someone or something will be killed, or great physical harm will come upon them. One lady recalled her baby being aborted for the purpose of sacrifice. When she screamed in horror, they told her that if she cried, another baby would die. As a result, she had not been able to cry for years. She was told to renounce that experience and renounce the lie that her crying would result in the death of anything or anyone. As soon as she did, she sobbed for several minutes.

When a teenager reaches adulthood, he/she may experience sexual dysfunction. Most Satanic rituals are violent sexual orgies, not sex as normal humans experience it. The ultimate high is sexual orgasm at the time of a kill. This is the stuff of extremely hardcore pornography, which is often linked to Satanism. Those who have been abused in this way need to renounce this sexual use of their bodies and forgive their sexual abusers. One victim clearly recalled 22 sexual abusers. Could we honestly expect them to forgive those multiple offenses? Yes, because God's faithfulness paves the way:

"He reached down from on high and took hold of me; he drew me out of deep waters. He rescued me from my powerful enemy, from my foes, who were too strong for me. They confronted me in the day of my disaster, but the Lord was my support. He brought me out into a spacious place; he rescued me because he delighted in me" (Psalm 18:16-19).

We encourage victims to renounce any suspected SRA, even when memories are blocked out or emotions are stifled.

How do we know that suspected SRA itself isn't a mind game or satanic deception?

One way is to look for any external confirmation. Never put suggested thoughts into a person's mind even if you suspect abuse because the mind is highly vulnerable to suggestions. The vague memory of an honest hug by a parent can be easily distorted into inappropriate fondling or worse. You should be suspicious of any details that come from a dream.

Nightmares usually indicate some spiritual assault but are generally eliminated after a person has found freedom in Christ. One girl accused her parents of sexual abuse because she had a dream, and a friend confirmed it through "words of knowledge." That is far too subjective a basis for making accusations. There will almost always be some external evidence confirming what is recalled.

Satan often attacks the minds of hurting people and seeks to discredit spiritual leaders by putting thoughts into their children's or associates' minds. We know of several cases where parents have been falsely accused by their children.

Counseling Forms

Sample Adult Counseling Consent Form

_____I understand that the staff of _____ Ministries and those associated with them are not professional or licensed counselors, therapists, medical or psychological practitioners, unless otherwise indicated.

_____I understand the persons leading these sessions are 'encouragers' in the Christian faith, who are helping me assume responsibility in finding freedom in Christ. I am also aware that my encourager may need to intervene if he or she suspects that a chid (under age of 18) or senior adult (over 65) is currently endangered by abuse or if I am a danger to myself or others.

_____I understand that I am not being advised to alter any prescription medication I am currently taking. This is a matter between myself and my physician/therapist.

_____I agree to be on time to appointment times. If I will be late or must cancel my scheduled appointment, I will make contact by phone to reschedule.

_____I understand that all information shared with my encourager is held in strict confidence. Information may be released if the individual expresses serious intent to harm himself/herself or someone else or there is evidence or reasonable suspicion of abuse against a minor child, elder person (over 65), or dependent adult.

_____I understand this counseling is free of charge. Many individuals ask what they may give. Partnership may look like $_____ initial partnership and $_____monthly partnership for _____months using the bank draft form on the back. Please give as God leads you. We thank you for partnering with _____Ministries.

_____I understand that after the introduction meeting the encourager will discuss with me the resource(s) needed and how many weeks we will be working together.

_____I understand that I will receive the following resources as our counseling material: EPIC Identity, Freedom and Journey workbooks; *Victory Over the Darkness, and The Bondage Breaker.*

_____I understand that I am here voluntarily and am free to leave at any time. I understand that my financial partnership will be adjusted depending on the number of meetings completed, should I leave early. I am also aware of my right to ask for clarification of any part of this statement.

_____I understand that all meetings unless otherwise changed by the encourager will take place at _____.

_____I understand the encourager will meet with me upon completion of the sessions to discuss next steps.

Name _____ Date _____

Address _____

City _____ State _____ Zip _____

Phone (Cell) _____ (Home)_____

Financial Support Options:

1. Bring a personal check to Freedom Appointment

2. If you would like to give electronically, you can enter your information below (Electronic transfer or Credit Card) or visit our website

Electronic Funds Transfer

I give my bank permission to transfer $ _____ from my personal account to

_____*Ministries each month beginning on:* _____

Name of payee_____ Phone _____

Address _____

City _____ State _____ Zip _____

Email _____

Bank Name _____ Bank Phone _____

Bank Account # _____ Bank Routing # _____

I prefer a monthly transfer date of: (circle one) **5th**   **10th**   **25th** of the month

Credit Card: *Visa   Discover   Master Card   American Express*

I give _____**Ministries** permission to charge my credit card $ _____
each month beginning on: _____.

Charge my card on (circle one) **5th**   **10th**   **25th** of the month

Card #_____ - _____ - _____ - _____

Expiration Date: _____   **Security code** (3 digits) _____

I have read, understand and agree with the information on this form. I understand that this authorization is in effect util I give written notices to _____ **Ministries** to either change or cancel payment method.

Signature _____

Sample Confidential Personal Inventory

Name _____ Cell Phone _____

Address _____

City _____ State _____ Zip _____

E-Mail _____

Marital Status_____

Preferred method of contact: □ E-mail   □ Cell phone

Please list the people who currently live in your home and relationship to you. _____

_____

Education: Highest Grade Completed_____Degrees earned_____

Vocation: Present:_____

                    Past:_____

Church Affiliation: Present_____

                              Past _____

Previous History of Marriage/Divorce: _____

Please describe why you are seeking help from Infusion Ministries at this time. _____

_____

_____

_____

Family History

Religious/Spiritual

Have any of your parents, grandparents, or great grandparents ever been involved in any occultist or non-Christian religious practices? Which ones?_____

_____

Briefly explain your parents' Christian experience (i.e., were they Christians and did they profess and live their Christianity?) If yes, explain. _____

_____

_____

_____

Relationships

Which of the following describes your parents? (Please check all that apply.)

☐ Married to each other   ☐ Father is remarried

☐ Divorced from each other   ☐ Mother divorced more than once

☐ Were never married to each other   ☐ Father divorced more than once

☐ Separated   ☐ Mother is deceased

☐ Mother is remarried   ☐ Father is deceased

Was there a sense of security and harmony in your home during the first 12 years of your life? Explain. _____

_____

_____

Who was the head of your childhood home? Explain. _____

_____

Describe the relationship between your parents during your childhood/adolescence._____

_____

Who was your primary caregiver during your childhood/adolescence? _____

_____

Who lived in your home with you when you were growing up? _____

_____

_____

Is there a history of adultery or incest anywhere in your family? Explain. _____

_____

_____

Is there a history of adoption or foster care within your family of origin? Explain. _____

_____

_____

Has anyone in your family been party to an abortion (male or female)? If yes, who? _____

_____

Has anyone in your family struggled with their sexual identity (gay, straight, bisexual) or gender identity (male, female, transgender)? Explain. _____

_____

Health

Describe any addictions in your family history (substance, sex, food, etc.). _____
_____
_____

Is there a history of mental illness anywhere in your family? If yes, explain. _____
_____
_____

Is there a history of any physical/medical conditions within your family? Explain._____
_____
_____

How would you describe your family of origin's concern for:

Diet _____

Exercise_____

Rest _____

Moral Climate

Regarding the first 18 years of your life, how would you rate the moral atmosphere in your home in terms of how you were parented? (circle one for each category)

Category	Overly Permissive	Permissive	Average	Strict	Overly Strict
Alcohol	5	4	3	2	1
Cigarettes	5	4	3	2	1
Clothing	5	4	3	2	1
Church Attendance	5	4	3	2	1
Dating	5	4	3	2	1
Illegal drug use	5	4	3	2	1
Literature	5	4	3	2	1
Movies	5	4	3	2	1
Music	5	4	3	2	1
Sex	5	4	3	2	1

Personal History

Physical

How would you describe your current personal concern for:

Diet _____

Exercise _____

Rest _____

Do you currently struggle with or have a personal history of addiction (substance, sex, food, etc.)? Explain. _____

_____

Have you ever undergone treatment for any addiction? Explain. _____

_____

_____

Do you currently have any physical / medical conditions for which you are receiving medical care? Explain. _____

_____

Please list any medications you are currently and consistently using. _____

_____

Do you have a personal history of any physical / medical conditions? Explain._____

_____

Describe your current sleep habits and sleep disturbances (ex. Recurring nightmares, insomnia, etc.) _____

_____

Do you currently take time for regular periods of rest and relaxation? Explain. _____

_____

Relationships

Are you adopted? _____

Which of the following have you experienced or participated in personally, or as a partner/spouse?

(Please check all that apply.)

☐ Abortion   ☐ Emotional abuse

☐ Miscarriage   ☐ Sexual abuse

☐ Still birth   ☐ Rape

☐ Live birth   ☐ Incest

☐ Verbal abuse   ☐ Spiritual abuse

☐ Physical abuse   ☐ Satanic ritual abuse

Please provide an explanation for any items that you marked above. _____
_____
_____

Have you ever personally struggled with your sexual identity (gay, straight, bisexual) or gender
identity (male, female, transgender)? Explain. _____
_____

Mental

Do you currently struggle with or have a personal history of any of the following? (mark all that apply)

☐ Daydreaming   ☐ Obsessive thoughts

☐ Lustful Thoughts   ☐ Insecurity

☐ Inferiority   ☐ Blasphemous thoughts

☐ Inadequacy   ☐ Compulsive behaviors

☐ Worry   ☐ Dizziness

☐ Doubts   ☐ Brain fog

☐ Fantasy   ☐ Other: _____

Have you ever spent time wishing you were somebody else, fantasizing that you were a different
person, or imagining yourself living at a different time, place, or under different circumstances?
Explain. _____
_____

About how much time do you spend each day on the following activities?

TV: _____ Video games: _____ Social Media/Internet: _____

Reading:_____

List your favorite TV programs, video games, websites/Apps and reading materials: _____

_____

What type(s) of music do you listen to? _____

_____

Would you consider yourself to be an optimist (tend to see the positives in people, situations) or a pessimist (tend to see the negative in people, situations)? Explain. _____

_____

Have you ever thought that maybe you were "going crazy," or do you currently fear that possibility? Explain. _____

_____

Have you ever been told that you have a mental disorder or mental illness? Explain. _____

_____

Have you ever or are you currently receiving therapy, counseling or treatment for a mental disorder or mental illness? Explain. _____

_____

Emotional

Have you ever or are you currently experiencing any of the following emotions on a regular basis? (mark all that apply).

☐	Frustration	☐	Hurt
☐	Anger	☐	Resentment
☐	Anxiety	☐	Fear of death
☐	Loneliness	☐	Fear of losing your mind
☐	Worthlessness	☐	Fear of committing suicide
☐	Depression	☐	Fear of hurting someone else
☐	Hatred	☐	Fear of terminal illness
☐	Bitterness	☐	Fear of going to hell
☐	Sadness	☐	Fear of (other)_____

Do you feel that any of the emotions (on the list on previous page) are sinful? Why?_____

_____

When you experience a difficult emotion, which of the following describes you? (Check all that apply.)

☐ I express emotions in a healthy way.

☐ I express emotions in an unhealthy way.

☐ I express some of my emotions, but not all.

☐ I acknowledge that I'm experiencing an emotion, but do not express it.

☐ I tend to suppress my emotions rather than acknowledge them.

☐ I find it safest not to express how I feel.

☐ I tend to disregard how I feel since I cannot trust my feelings.

☐ I consciously or subconsciously deny my emotions; it's too painful to deal with them.

☐ I am unsure or unaware of what I actually feel.

☐ I am not sure if the way I express my emotions is healthy or unhealthy.

Is there someone in your life right now with whom you could be emotionally honest (i.e. you could tell this person exactly how you feel about yourself, life, and other people)? Explain. _____

_____

_____

Do you feel that you can be emotionally honest with God? Explain. _____

_____

Spiritual

Do you know where you will spend eternity after you die? _____ Why do you believe that?_____

_____

Suppose you died tonight and found yourself standing before God. How would you answer if He asked you, "Why should I let you into Heaven?" _____

_____

_____

First John 5: 11-12, says, "God has given us eternal life, and this life is in his Son. He who has the Son has life; he who does not have the Son of God does not have life." Do you have the Son of God in you (I Corinthians 15:3-4)?_____

_____

Approximately when did you receive him (John 1:12)?_____

How do you know that you have received him? _____

_____

Do you have doubts or concerns regarding salvation? Explain. _____

_____

_____

_____

Are you presently enjoying fellowship with other believers? Explain._____

_____

_____

Are you currently a member of a local church? _____

    If yes, which church? _____

    If yes, are you attending regularly? _____

    If yes, do you support your church with your time, talent and treasure? _____

    If you answered "NO" to any of the above questions, please explain. _____

_____

Which of the following describe your personal spiritual lifestyle? (check all that apply)

☐ I read the Bible regularly.   ☐ I pray regularly.

☐ I read the Bible occasionally.   ☐ I pray occasionally.

☐ I do not read the Bible.   ☐ I do not pray.

When attending church or experiencing other Christian ministries, are you or have you ever been plagued with foul thoughts, jealousies, or other mental harassments? Explain. _____

_____

_____

EPIC Events

Our passion at Infusion Ministries is to train pastors and other leaders to help their people understand what it means to be a child of God and walk in freedom from destructive habits. We provide training and resources for all ages and groups. In addition to the summits below, we have training tailored to parents, small group leaders and others. Contact us for more details and how you can join us in Knoxville, TN, for a summit, or bring these powerful truths to your church or ministry. Call (865) 966-1153, or visit infusionnow.org for the most up to date information on our events.

EPIC Summit

This three-day summit is held live in Knoxville, TN, and broadcast on ZOOM in the spring and fall, and consists of three parts:

- **Identity:** EPIC Identity material walks us through the biblical truths about who we are in Christ and how to replace the negative, false ideas we have believed about ourselves with these truths.

- **Freedom:** Satan wants to keep us in bondage to destructive habits, addictions, fear, anger, unforgiveness and more. But Jesus came to set us free. EPIC Freedom provides tools to win the battle for the mind and live in his freedom.

- **The Lord's Prayer Journey:** We utilize the Lord's Prayer as a means for the Holy Spirit to reveal any doors opened to the enemy, unresolved spiritual conflict or unforgiveness and help us claim freedom.

EPIC Leadership Summits

This two-day summit is held live and broadcast via ZOOM in Knoxville, TN, once a year.

- **EPIC Leader I:** So many leaders do not feel qualified or equipped to help those with spiritual conflicts and bondage. EPIC Leader I provides Biblical tools and principles that will help you bring the message of identity and freedom in Christ to your church or organization.

- **EPIC Leader II:** Provides material that will give you a clear model and guide to discipleship counseling and tools to help all believers overcome their spiritual conflicts.

EPIC Latino Summit

This is a five-day summit, held live in Knoxville, TN, once a year in late summer, and may be broadcast on ZOOM. EPIC Identity, Freedom and Journey are combined with EPIC Leadership 1 and Leadership 2 materials - all presented in Spanish. Contact us for information on the next EPIC Latino Summit.

EPIC Christian Adventures

This outdoor camp experience for men is to help them discover their true identity and freedom in Christ so they can live as the men God has made them to be. You will enjoy excellent meals, hiking and fishing and the opportunity to encounter God without the distractions of daily life. To learn about our next adventure, call Infusion Ministries at 865-966-1153 or visit infusionnow.org.

The Holy Land Tour, led by Dr. Dave Park

During this life-altering journey, usually in May or June, we tour numerous natural, civic and religious sites described in scriptures and share in meaningful times of worship, instruction, and prayer. To find out more information about the next trip, visit our website at infusionnow.org.

Made in the USA
Columbia, SC
20 January 2021